MW01504116

After years of research and trillions of dollars, scientists have accomplished what many thought would be impossible. They have combined the fun of floral shapes and the education of cursing into one glorious, revolutionary coloring book.

No need to color and wonder how you can insult someone at your favorite sports bar. No need to worry about stress relief and learning phrases that would even make a sailor blush. And there is no need to wonder if you only color because you suck at art. (You do) We have saved marriages, united countries and healed the ozone. Our gift from the heavens is truly the greatest educational art book of all time.

So, if you are seeking to improve your art skills, relieve anxiety or learn how to curse with the foreign exchange student, no matter how you cut it. We got you covered.

Disclaimer : Our content was translated into either the literal meaning, overall intent of the phrase or a local expression that doesn't make sense to foreigner

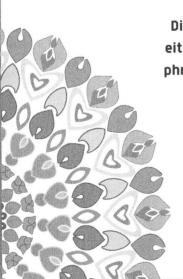

MAMABICHO

Dick Sucker

Spanish
Puerto Rico

FRANDSEROIR

Uncle Fucker

Icelandic

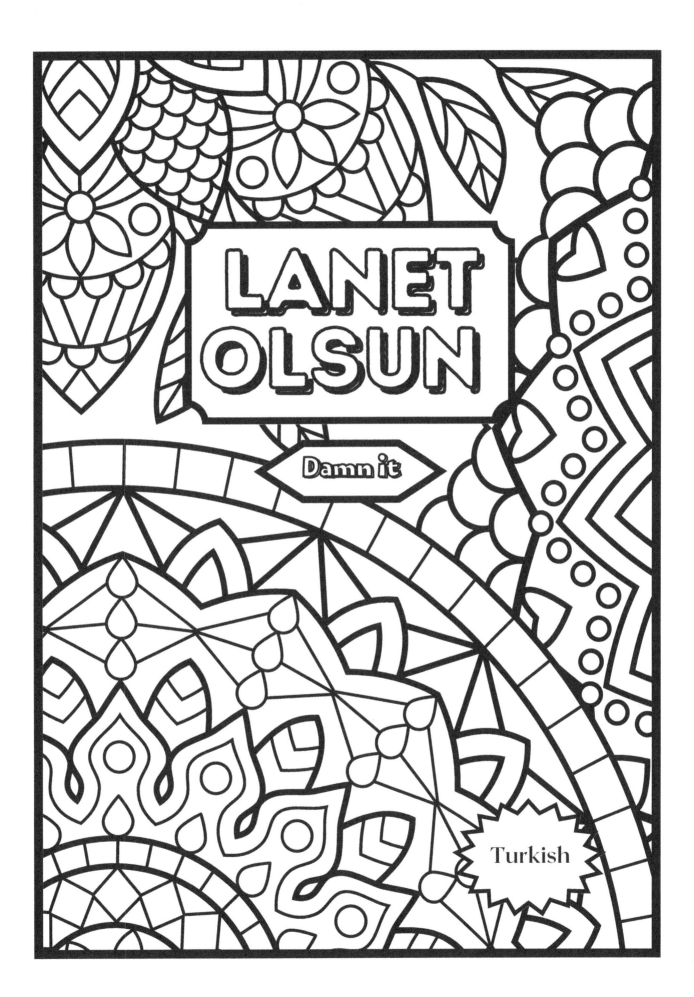

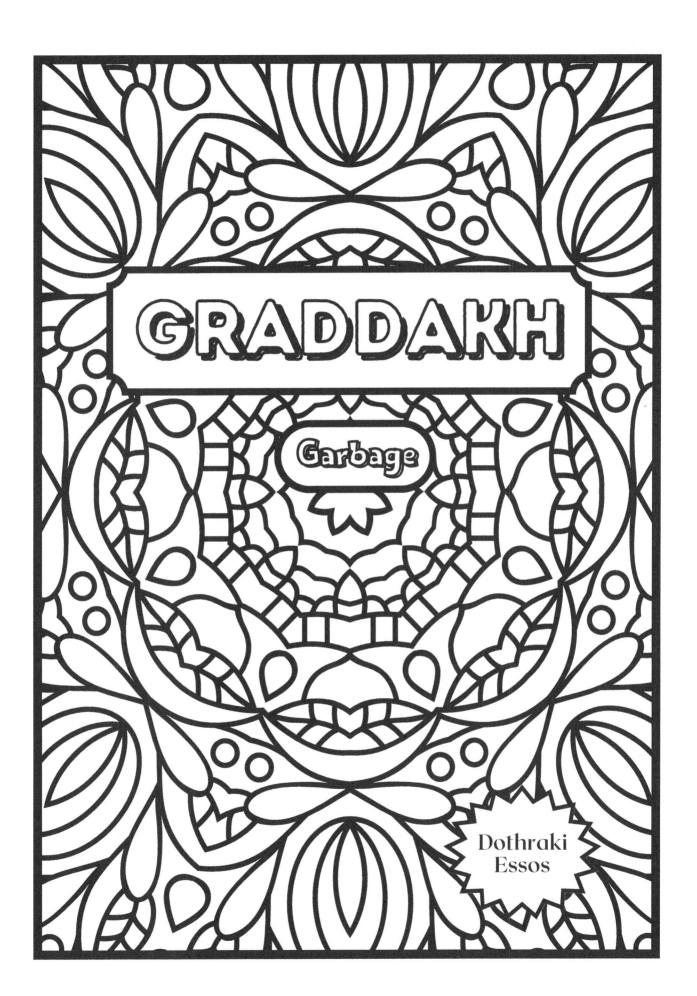

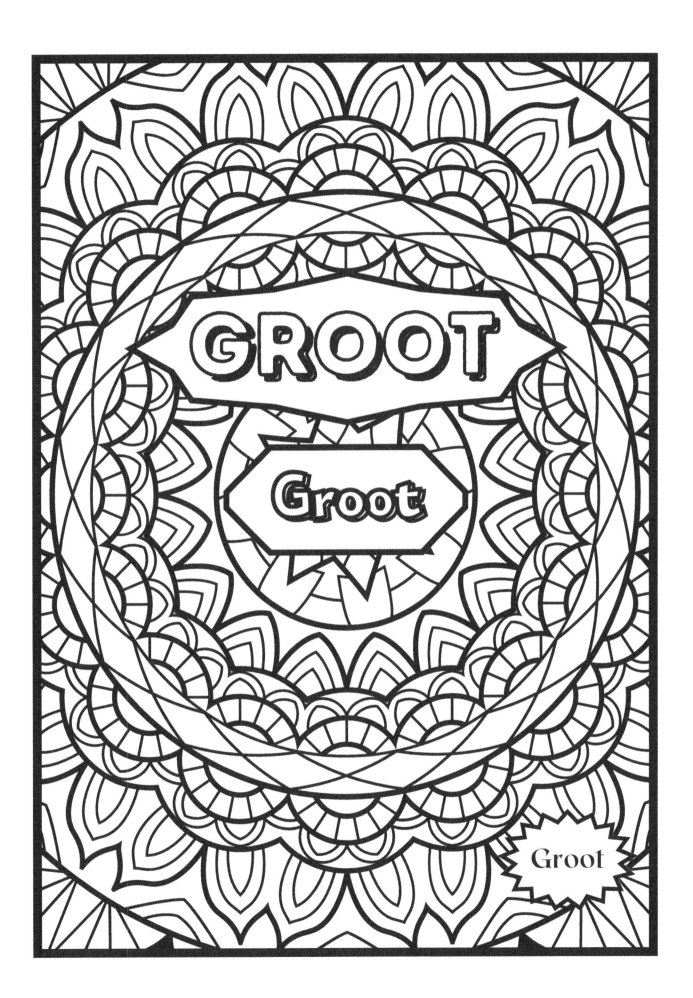

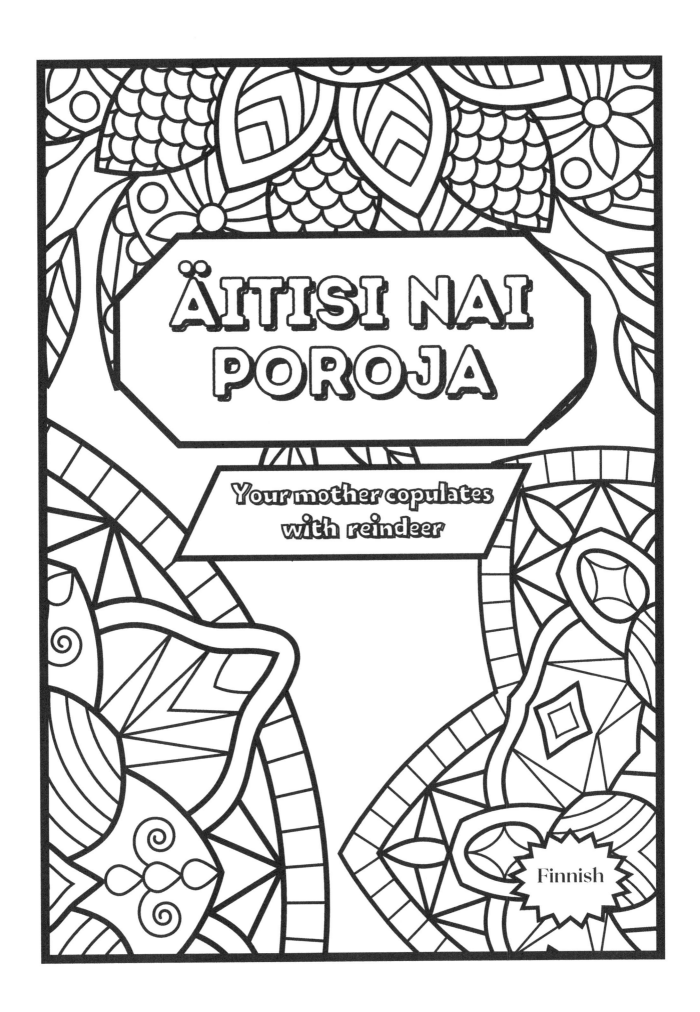

ÄITISI NAI POROJA

Your mother copulates with reindeer

Finnish

PEEDUNKY

Punk

Huttese

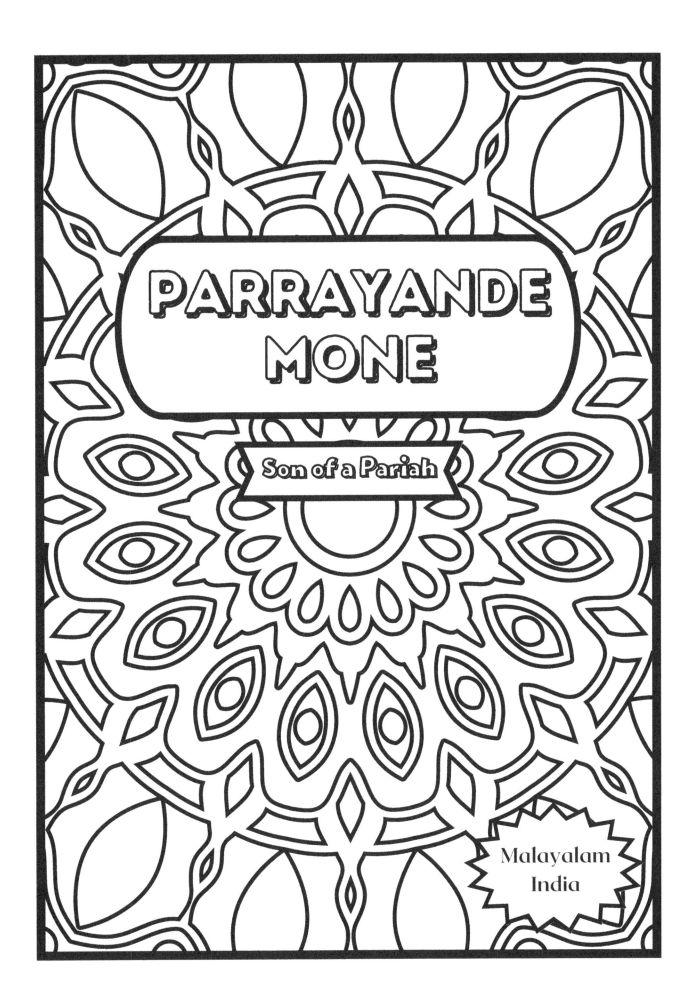

PARRAYANDE MONE

Son of a Pariah

Malayalam
India

HEE HOO NEIGH

Your mom is a horse

Donkey

VAI CEIFAR BATATAS

Go dig potatoes

Portuguese Brazil

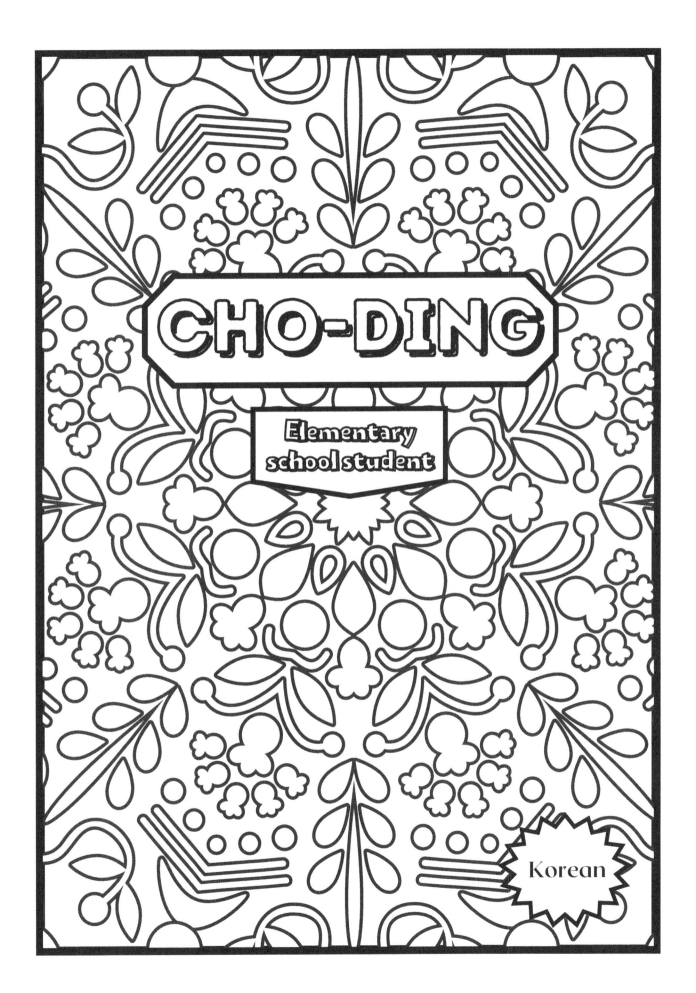

CHO-DING

Elementary school student

Korean

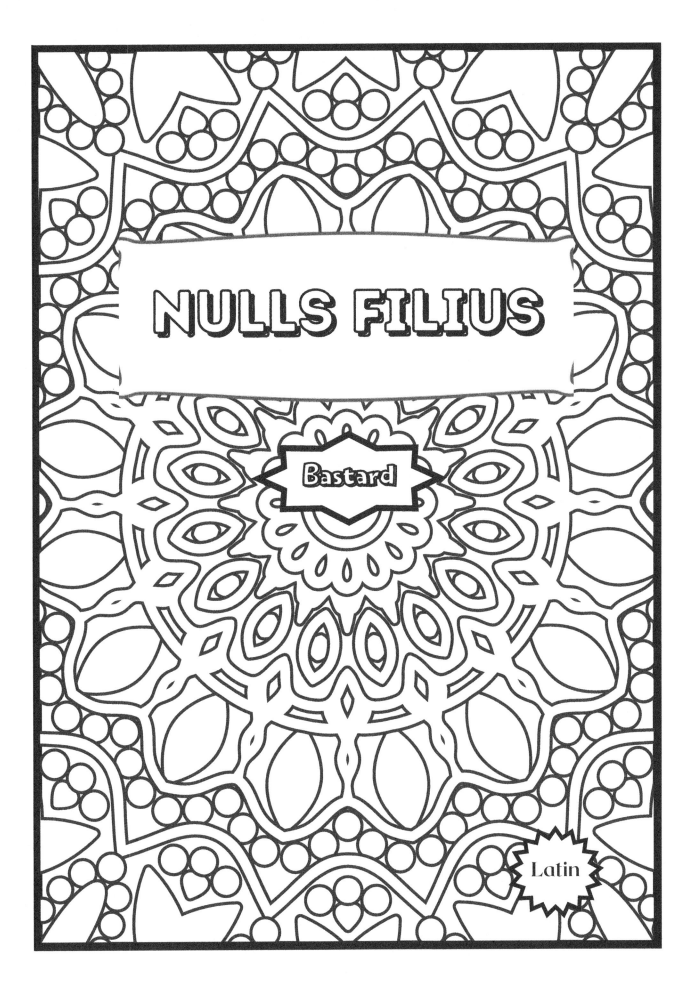

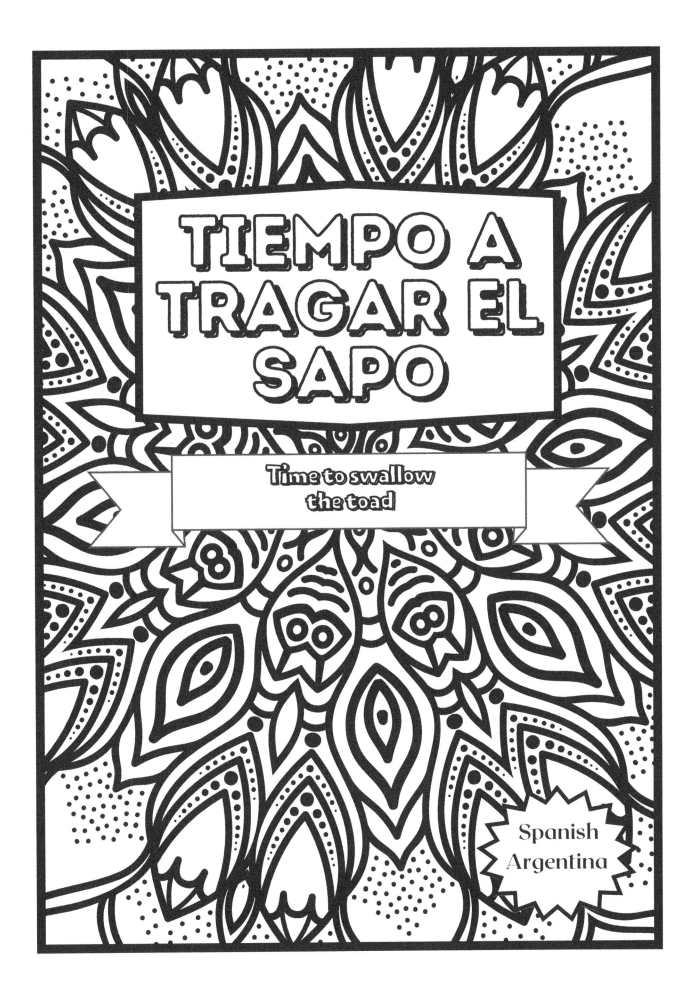

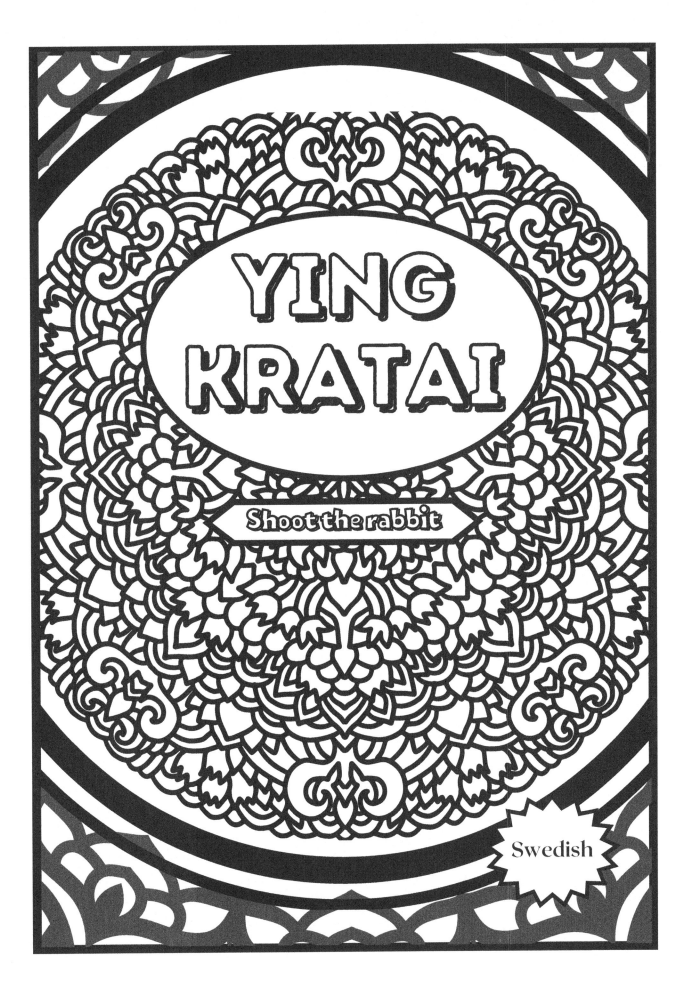

KOR-E KHAR

Son of a donkey

Persian

BAHAAYIM

Livestock

Arabic

KUSE MUUNTAJAAN

May you piss into a transformer

Finnish

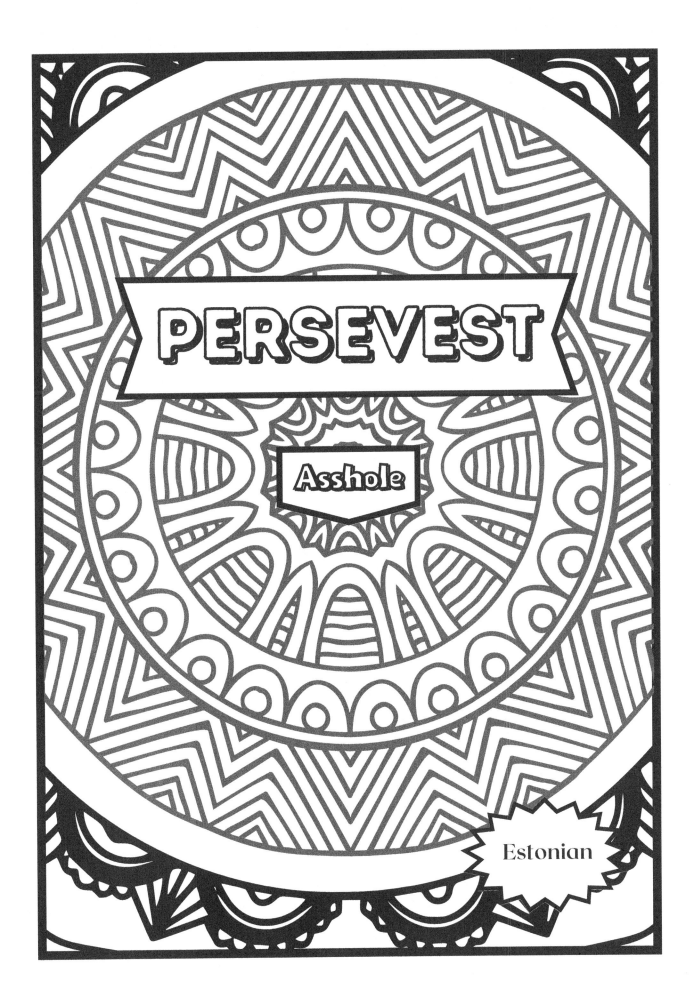

TARU NAKKHOD JAI

May destruction befall you

Gujarati
India

SHINJIMAE

May you drop dead

Japanese

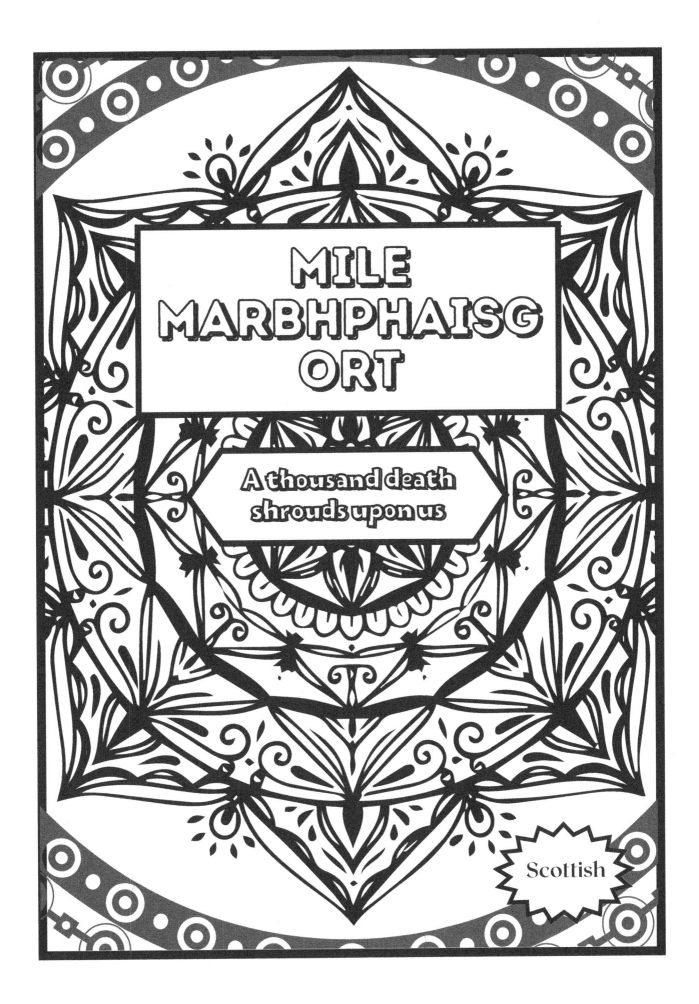

IMEACHT GAN TEACHT ORT

Damn your family and its place of origin

Irish

KRIJG HET LAZARUS

May you go catch Leprosy

Dutch

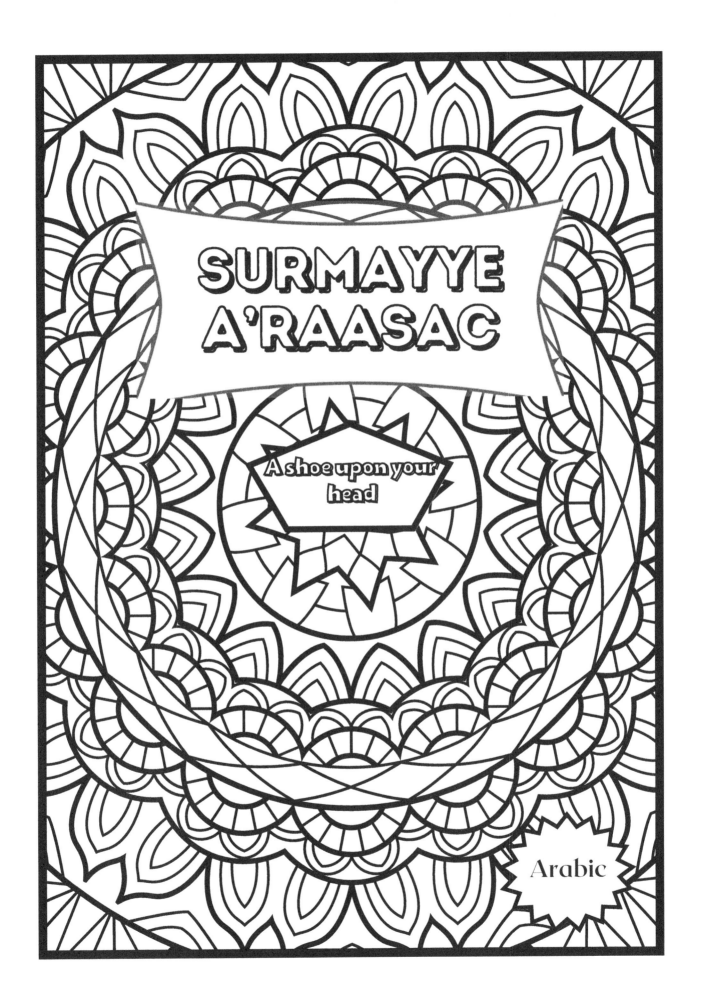

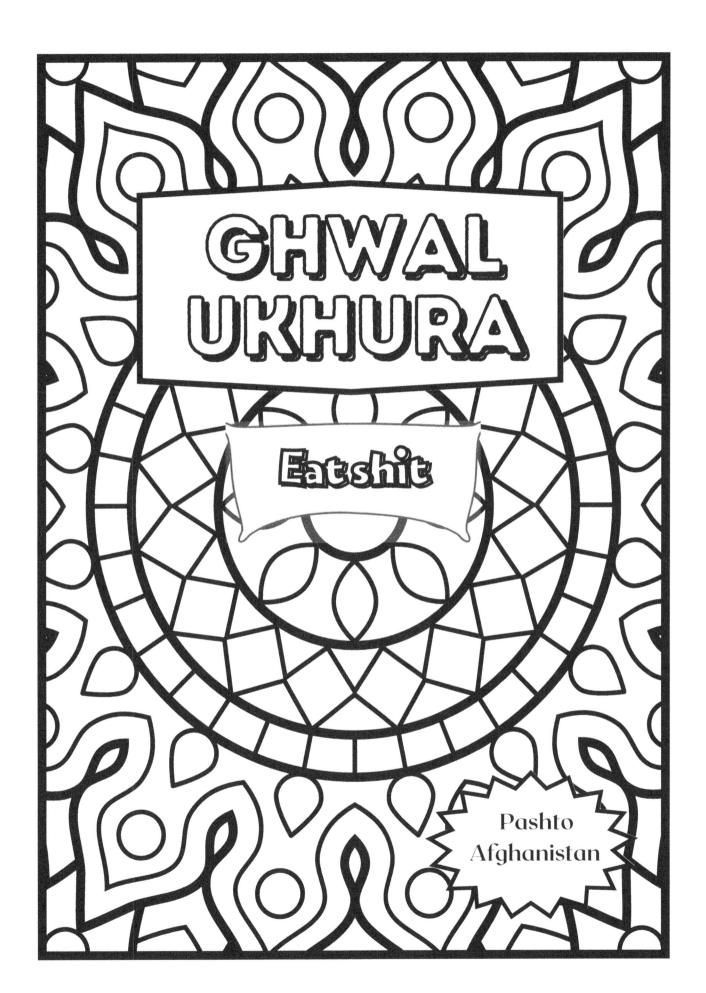

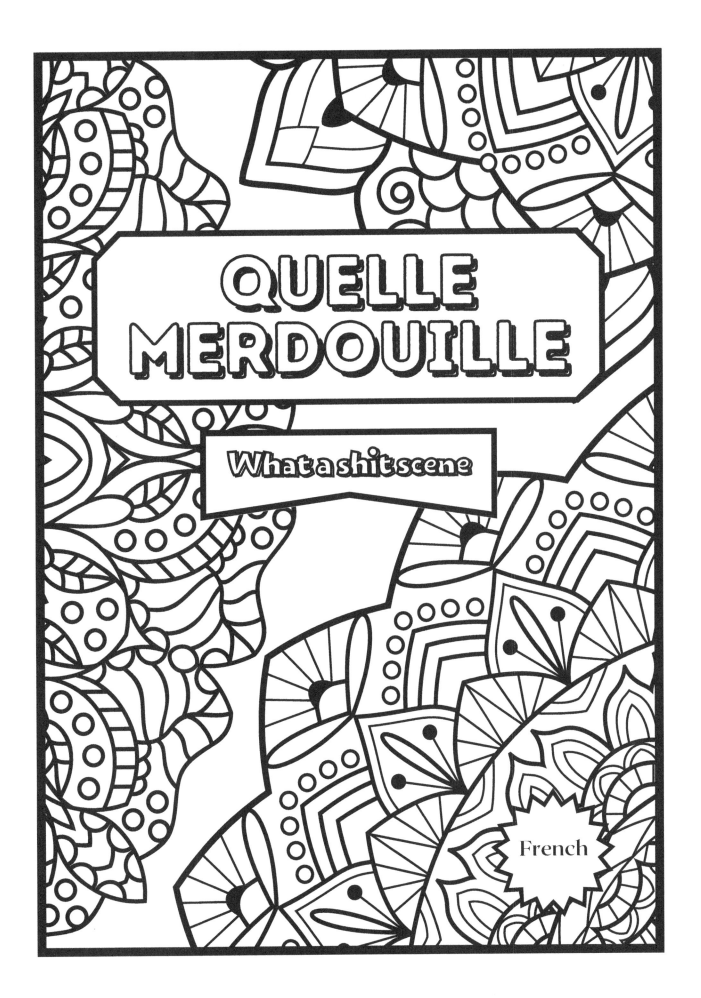

SHRAMA SAKHO

A skidmark on your underwear

Xhosa
Africa

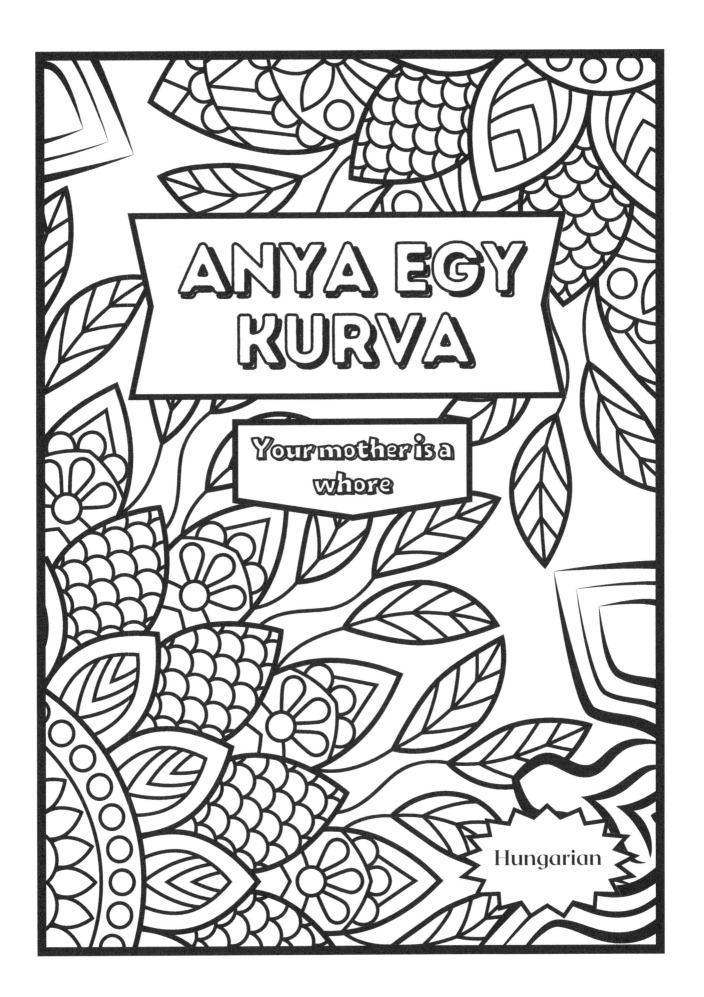

EICH MAM A YW A HEN SGUTHAN

Your mother is an old wood pigeon

Welsh

PICHKATA LELINA

Your aunt's nether regions

Bulgarian

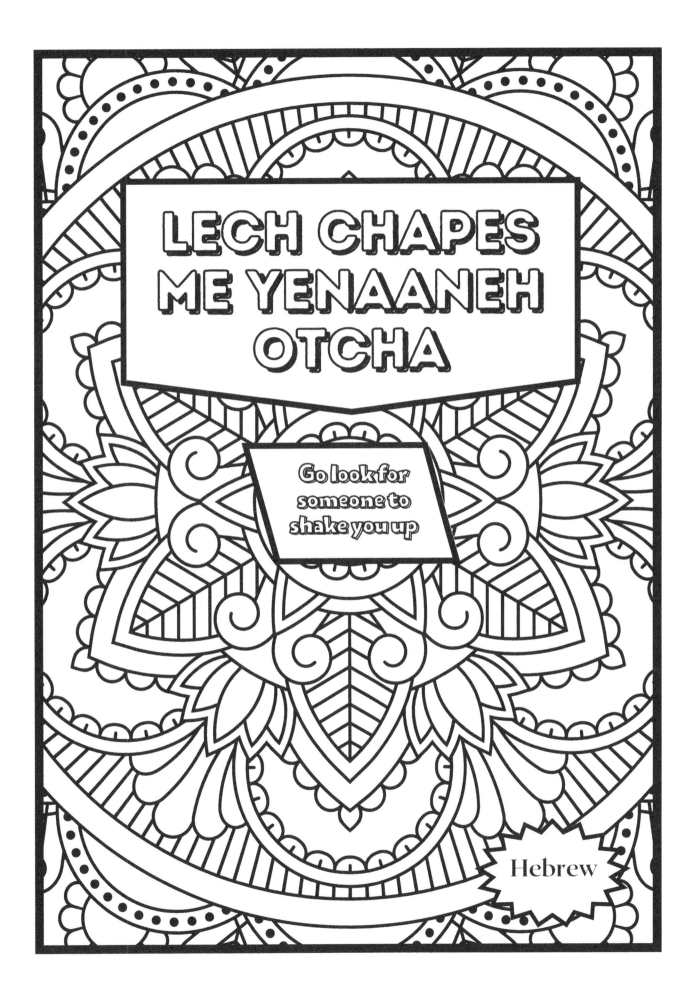

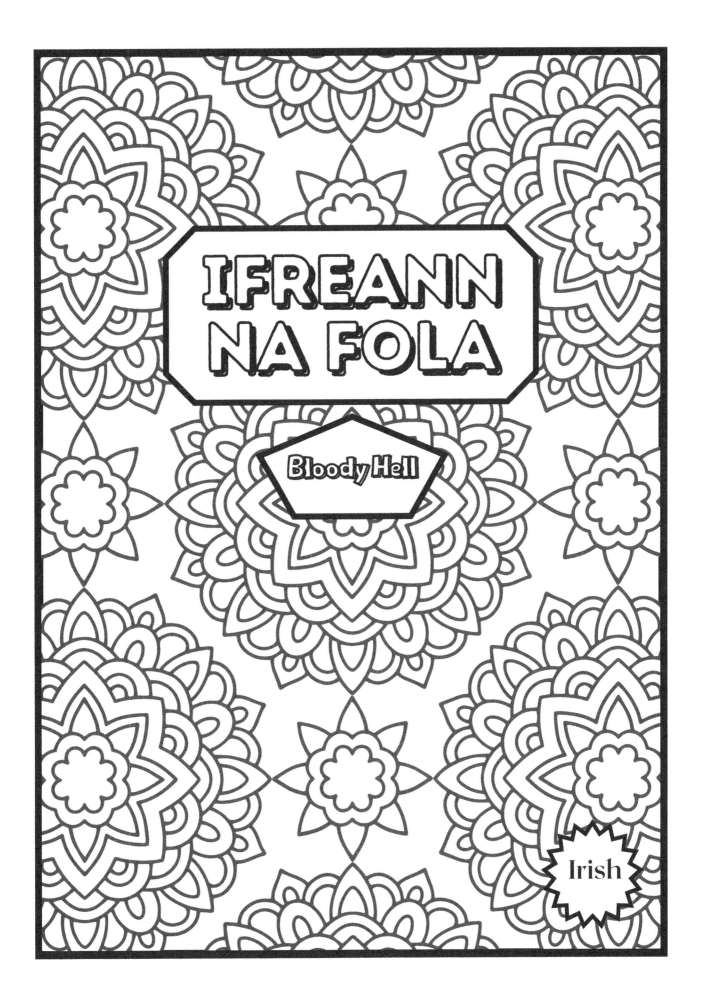

Made in the USA
Monee, IL
29 January 2023

26197798R00090